Happily Ever After

Living the Golden Years With Your Partner

By Lita Caine

Table of Contents

Introduction

Congratulations! You have successfully entered the decade that marks your *Golden Years.* If you ask us, when you have been married for 50 years, you have successfully found the key to true happiness. The fact that a couple made it so far is commendable because not everyone can stick to the commitment they made when saying the *"I dos."*

You have loved, and you are living a wonderful life together! So, what's left? Granted that you're not newlywed. You have kids and grandkids. Does that mean you should not show that you found love? Doesn't your spouse deserve the same attention when you first met?

Nowadays, when you ask a couple, "How long has it been since you got married?" They answer with, "We got married six years ago."

You know what would be an appropriate response – "It feels like yesterday."

Can you imagine the smile this simple statement will bring on your spouse's face? They would be ecstatic that you still believe that your love is the same as it was when you first met.

Here's some food for thought — you found your partner when you had almost given up on love. Through thick and thin, you stick by their side. You dedicated decades to each other, learned everything about each other's likes and dislikes, you had crazy sex, fought, and made up... it was a wild ride.

Are you with us so far? In all areas, YOU ROSE ABOVE. A balance was maintained and the best years of your life were lives with someone you loved and respected. You have loved them with your whole heart and now that you are feeling a little wobbly, you feel there's trouble in paradise?

Sorry to break it to you but this happens to the best of us. Just because a little doubt has entered your mind, it doesn't mean that your love for your spouse has dimmed. It's probably something niggling in the back of your mind that you can't put your finger on.

All you need to do is remember that time when you first met and made the promise to stay with each other forever. Let the good moments sprinkle in with a dash of the bad ones that you came out of fighting and winning as a couple... and there you have it — the secret to living the *Golden Years*.

Reality and Expectations

All couples go into marriage with certain expectations. The words "forever" and "lifetime" are thrown around whenever the said topic is the main point of discussion. Those who have successfully made it to their retirement as a couple define marriage that has lasted the test of time as long-term monogamy.

We expect that we will grow old with our spouse surrounded by feelings such as passion, a deep connection, romance, and desire.

Think of it as the ingredients to the love recipe. What happens when you eat your pie? The lingering sweetness makes your heart want more even when your stomach is full. What we are trying to say is that growing old is about feeling content like that sweetness that stays in your mouth for a while.

Young couples are always seesawing between realistic and unrealistic expectations. The former are those that you rightly deserve and the latter are those that you just want because they will help you achieve celebrity couple goals.

Your bond does get stronger with these feelings but it does not last forever. Sometimes, romance gets left behind when you enter your *Golden Years* and that's alright because when you grow in a relationship, the journey starts with love and evolves into friendship. This is good when you are older and have a grandson to play with.

You need to realize that whether 5 years have passed after your marriage or 50, your spouse won't remain the same person. They will grow and change in ways you might not have imagined. Some you will like and others you will have to make peace with. The more open you are to these changes, the fewer problems you will have. These changes encompass physical appearance, mental health, emotional state, etc.

No matter at what stage you stand, it's never too late to realize your mistake. There will always be ups and downs in a relationship. How you handle them determines the longevity of your relationship.

Habits of Successful Couples

Ignorance makes things a little bit cloudy and complicated. With it in the way, you are unable to see the strong bond you have with your partner. This rough patch you are experiencing right now is because lately, you have been taking your relationship for granted.

Why not stop for a minute and think about its cause. Did you know that all old married couples stay with each other for the same reasons? No, this is not a sarcastic statement that will make you spin in circles. If you ask any person, husband or wife, they will list down the following reasons behind their successful relationship:

Be With Your Spouse for the Right Reasons

Your friend has been trying to set you up on a date for a very long time. You finally agreed and met the person at a restaurant. After a few minutes of talking, you realize that you both have nothing in common. The next day your friend calls you to get the deets and you say that you guys didn't click. Your friend argues that the person is nice and that you should give them a chance. Your second date went a little better and those turned into regular meetings and before you knew it, you were moving in together. The person then proposed and you said yes. Now, it has been 25 years since your marriage, and sometimes, you still wonder why you married the person because all they provide is security.

The promise of a comfortable life is more dangerous than love because those who are not romantic are only looking for someone they can settle down with. This is why it's important to be together for the right reasons.

For instance, you were raised as a Catholic, and getting married was what one was supposed to do. Wrong! You felt lonely and miserable and thought that having someone in your life will fix everything. Wrong!

The only reason you should marry someone is that you like to be in their company. When you talk to them, it brings a smile to your face. It's that simple!

Ask anyone who has married twice or thrice and they will tell you the following:

I married for the first time for the wrong reasons. These reasons include:

- Family pressure
- Meddlesome friends
- Feeling like I haven't accomplished anything and I am a loser because I settled for the first person I met
- I married because it boosted my social image and we both looked good as a couple
- I was naïve and young, and irrevocably in love (Team Edward or Team Jacob?)

A relationship does not fix you. You might get a slight reprieve in the beginning but you won't ever be able to reach those *Golden Years*.

Now that you know the secret behind reaching the *Golden Years*, let's talk about the habits that successful people have:

They Adapt to and Embrace the Changes Their Spouse Develop

You married your partner because they were career-driven. You both were on the same page and that's what you bonded over. As your relationship progressed, your career got sidelined, and staying committed to each other became more important. When you got married, things like saving for a honeymoon, buying a house, and starting a family got all your attention.

As more things changed in your relationship, so did your spouse's priorities. After a while, you noticed that you and your spouse were no longer on the same page. You both were pursuing different things.

A successful couple does not operate in this manner. For them, compromise is everything! They know everything about their spouse and not only that but they also regularly check in with them to know if there's something they need or want to talk about.

They notice every little change from their spouse developing a sudden liking to Chinese food to anything major such as working hard to buy something they have been wanting for quite some time. They don't bicker when one of them prioritizes something because they understand.

Remember — your spouse's goals are your goals and vice-versa. Share their dreams and stand by their side and expect the same from them. That's how successful couples write the story of their relationship.

They Are Affectionate

Did you tease your spouse in the initial days after your marriage when watching TV? Did you hold their hand and tried to kiss them because you weren't in the mood to watch a show? What about now? Do you still do it? If no then why not?

Perhaps, you are going through something stressful but if this has become a routine then the distance in your relationship will slowly grow into a wide gap.

We understand that people show affection in different ways such as giving your spouse a massage because they are exhausted or doing the house chores because they are working on a project that's on deadline. From making their favorite tea to bringing a bouquet and chocolates for no reason, these are the little things that make every person happy. You don't need to be a young couple to do this. The fact that you are old and still have a young heart is what keeps a relationship going.

Fight Fair

Angry door slams, name-calling, not saying a word to each other… if that's what your relationship has come to then you need to act fast. These situations are faced more by young couples than old couples. Older couples have learned the art of fighting fair. They know that fighting on something baseless will only result in hurtful words said from both sides.

Plus, older couples have had their fair share of fights. Now that they know absolutely everything about each other, they seldom fight because there are no secrets. When couples get old, any fights they have are not about winning or losing. They are more about sharing different opinions and accepting the fact that even though they love each other, there are still some things they disagree on.

Imagine how easy it would become to take your relationship to the next level only if you realized that despite your beliefs and opinions clashing, you respect each other's point of view.

Their Communication is Strong

Most couples don't realize the importance of communication. It is "THE" key to surviving in a relationship. When married couples don't communicate, they try to either ignore or control each other/ In *Rachel's* words, "How do you expect me to grow, if you won't let me blow."

Remember the time when you couldn't wait to talk to your partner and share every single detail of anything that happened to you in the day?

At this stage of life, that intense communication has turned to having a pleasant chat over dinner, watching TV, and commenting on the acting being lame, etc. Just because there isn't anything exciting to share doesn't mean that your relationship is going stale. If you ask us — it's going perfect! Your relationship has come to a point where you can talk about anything and everything, even if it sounds silly in your head.

They Don't Run Away from the Physical Changes of Aging

When you married your partner, you both were in your primes and had well-maintained bodies. With time, this changed. There are a dozen scenarios here that could take place and test you such as, you got news about your spouse being sick and requiring around-the-clock care. So, do what you can to make sure that your spouse lives a happy life.

Or, your spouse developed amnesia and can no longer remember you. Would you leave her just because she can no longer recall the love you shared? The movie "The Vow" is described as *the tale of love that refuses to be forgotten*. In the movie, Channing Tatum promises his on-screen wife Rachel McAdams that no matter what might happen, he will always love her. Yet, she's the one who forgets him and goes back to her first fiancé. Tatum tries repeatedly to convince her of their love and she refuses him at every turn. In the end, it's their love that brings them closer and not their memories.

The point of telling you this is that when you love someone, you accept them as a whole. From small changes in their body to their food choices and things that change drastically, none of these will matter if you truly love your partner.

The challenges of aging are plenty and handling them can be… what's the right word for it — exhausting, perhaps. However, if you give your best and realize that things are not that different from when you became one, the rest of your life will be spent comfortably.

The Answer to Your Burning Question – What Makes Love Last?

How many times have you heard the word "love" being described as "forever?"

You have probably lost count. Well, the truth is — love does not last forever but marriage sure does.

Most people say to themselves, "I can make my marriage work but how do I stay true to the promise of forever?"

You will be amazed to know the answer — it's all in the little details.

In movies and romance novels, when the main character makes a mistake, their best friend says, "Go big or go home." What the hero or heroine does next is hella romantic. Things get back to normal again and the characters finally marry and... live happily after?

No. You see, couples fight. To make it to the Golden Years with squabbles that don't destroy your relationship, you need to keep the small things in mind. For example, you and your spouse are fighting over a matter. After a while, you somehow ended the fight and made up. After a few days, another fight breaks out, and it's similar to the last one. The cycle repeats — you end the fight and make up.

Do you think this is healthy? The second, third or fourth fight will never happen if you resolve the first one with communication and not compromise. So, how does one put the squabbles to rest?

The following advice will help you understand how a simple touch and words can change things:

Cuddle Time Lasts Forever

Who doesn't love cuddles? When you are having a bad day, walking into the arms of your partner can be the stress-reliever you need. Those two engulfing arms simply make everything better.

Sneak in cuddles anytime you can — while watching TV, in bed, when making breakfast, on the porch when watching the sun set, etc.

Think of every cuddle opportunity as a moment that will bring you closer than ever to each other.

Don't Leave Your Spouse in Bed

Ahem, ahem… what we are trying to say is that instead of getting out of bed and getting ready for work, what now stay in for a while. Cuddle your spouse and watch them open their eyes. Switch up your mornings by designating breakfast days, complete each other's chores, and do those little things that free up more room for you two to spend time together.

It often happens that when you start your 3rd or 4th decade in marriage, you don't pay much attention to routines. You start to do your own thing, which is good for you but sharing a routine helps build harmony.

One Thank You Is Not Enough

Ask your spouse and they will tell you how many times you have acted like a complete idiot and a jerk. In this case, instead of apologizing for your mistake or behavior, why not *thank* them for keeping up with you. Handling the crazy side of you is no easy task, even if you know that. The fact that they love you for who you are is something you should always cherish. This is why a dozen thank you in a day is a must.

For example, it's the weekend and you and your spouse decided to go out, watch a movie and have dinner. Suddenly, an old friend calls you and says that they would love to meet up because they are in the city only for a day. Instead of calling your spouse, you text her saying the plan is canceled. When your spouse does not reply to you, you realize things won't be good for you when you get back home.

You get home at 11:00 P.M. and find your spouse in bed, watching TV. You walk up to them, kiss them on the cheek, and say, "Thank you for letting me spend the day with my friend. I promise I will make it up to you. I love you."

Did you notice that we didn't mention the word "sorry?" That's because *sorry* tells a story about patterns and this is not something that you want to define your relationship with. However, keep in mind that a "thank you" does not always work. Sometimes hip. In fact, you will be in the dog house.

Accept Their Apology

A mistake was made and now your spouse is apologizing. It's alright to be angry but holding on to this intense feeling can destroy your relationship.

When you first started dating your now-spouse, you probably apologized at every turn. When you got committed to each other, you would fight and then apologize. When you got married, fights became a problem. You probably thought to yourself, "He/she has known me for years then can she/he make this mistake?"

Fights will forever stay in your relationship. Fighting is healthy because it shows that you are working out your problems. However, when you fail to resolve your fights, that's when the relationship turns toxic.

So, when you fight with your spouse, instead of saying "I am sorry" or "It's fine," table the matter. When you are ready to talk, have open, honest communication and when your spouse gets your point of view, thank them for understanding you.

Plan Extraordinary Gestures

Your spouse follows a ritual — waking up every morning, freshening up, making breakfast, waking you up, having breakfast together, and then going back to finishing their little DIY project. Why not take their place now and then? Wake you early, freshen up, and have breakfast in bed. Let them stay in for a while until you get their work things ready. While eating, sprinkle a little salt on your partner's food because you know that's how they like it.

Turning their simple ritual into an extraordinary one by starting the morning for them is a great way to bring a smile to their face. There are plenty of things you can do to turn their frown upside down or simply make them happy. Just remember that the gesture can be small or big, but it should touch their heart.

Doesn't this seem like the simplest advice to follow? Even though it is, consistency can be a little demanding. However, if you love your spouse and want to show them that you don't just care about them but they mean the world to you then you need to put in a lot of effort and that starts with being consistent. Never do these things out of obligation because they will start to feel like a burden. Do them from your heart. Don't do them for praise but to improve the latent bond between you and your spouse.

Space Over Sex? Making Your Relationship Last Longer

Did you know that sex in older couples is dictated by their personality? A study published in the journal of *Archives of Sexual Behavior*, individuals who have a positive outlook on life and in social situations, have sex frequently, whether it may be with their spouse or partner. The numbers are high in men because of two factors: believing that sex is important and thinking about sex.

That's men for you in a nutshell. However, this begs the question, "Is space more important than sex when you reach the Golden Years?"

Kids and adults don't like to think about their parents having sex. Through grandparents in the mix most people assume that they lead a pretty boring life.

Here's another revelation that will shock you. According to a study published in the *Journal of Marriage and Family*, sex in midlife and older couples is characterized by the changes that take place over time. For couples between the ages 50 and 69, the distress came from age-related changes that manifested differently in both genders. For older couples between the ages of 70 and 86, emotional intimacy took precedence over sex. The study concluded that even though sex is the cause of conflict in married couples, later life wives and husbands have more congruent marital sex.

From this information, you can deduce that neither sex nor space is needed for a long-lasting relationship. To answer your question, *happiness* is the secret to making it to the Golden Years.

If you are happy with your spouse and your life then you know how to handle any challenge that makes its way into your marriage. However, this does not mean that you should discard space… for space is the path to happiness.

Understanding Why Space Matters In a Relationship

Having enough privacy and space in a relationship allows couples to be happy. The formula is that simple! Some people might see it as abandonment but spouses who feel secure in their marriage and know that their partner loves them don't feel this way.

For example, Stephen and Laurel just had a baby. In the first few months, they both struggled as a parent. Stephen saw how exhausted Laurel was feeding the baby day and night, working from home, and doing house chores. As for Laurel, she felt she wasn't giving Stephen enough time and lately, they hadn't had any date night. The problem was they couldn't take out time from their hectic schedule. Stephen would come home from work, play with their baby a little, have dinner with Laurel and go to sleep. Laurel would then stay up late cleaning the house and catching up on projects that she had to leave in the middle when her baby was crying. When their daughter turned 8 months old, a couple of Stephen's colleagues asked him if he would like to join them on a mountain expedition. Stephen reluctantly asked Laurel if he could go on the trip and she said yes. She knew how important this was to Stephen because he had always been an outdoor enthusiast, and apart from their honeymoon period, they hadn't vacationed in 6 years. Stephen asked Laurel how she would manage and she said, "Looking after myself and just the baby is the space I need to feel a little unburdened and I have friends and family who will drop everything and come running at my word."

If this story sounds still a little bit off to you then perhaps what we are about to tell you next will convince you.

A psychologist, research professor, and the author of *Finding Love Again: 6 Simple Steps to a New and Happy Relationship*, Dr. Terri Orbuch says that married couples who last longer know the importance of space. Her project *The Early Years of Marriage* has been going on for 30 years. The project began in 1990 and had 373 married couples at the start. In the span of 25 years, 46% of them divorced.

29% of the spouses told Dr. Orbuch that they didn't have enough "private time for themselves." 31% of the wives reported that their husbands didn't give them any free time, whereas 26% of the husbands reported the same thing. 11.5% of couples reported being unhappy and their reason was they had no privacy for themselves. This percentage was higher than the 6% of couples who reported that they were unhappy due to their sex life.

There were a couple of other factors that affected the outcome. These included control, well-being, marital stability, competence, happiness, equality, couple similarity, styles of interactions, closeness with family, conflict management, traditionality in roles, household labor division, and compatibility in orientation.

Dr. Orbuch concluded that space is "THE" surviving factor in a relationship!

In our opinion, spouses who get alone time to themselves can follow their interests, which makes them happy. Those spouses, who depend on each other too much, tend to be clingy and have a boring relationship.

So, we can safely say that having an appropriate amount of time to yourself that allows you to pursue what you love, makes your relationship stronger and last longer. Remember: Demanding space does not mean that you are neglecting your responsibilities. It simply means that you just want to be and by yourself for a while to quiet your mind.

Tips on How to Make Your Marital Relationship Last Longer

Making your marriage last longer is different than saving it. The former is about increasing your level of bonding and love and the latter is about a spouse convincing their partner they love them. The most common reason behind divorce is that people change over time and when a spouse is not able to notice those changes, they feel as if they have lost their partner. One of them is living in the present and the other one is living in the past.

When older couples grow apart, it's because they have relied on the past too much and have grown comfortable with what they know. This isn't anything big that can't be fixed with communication. In this situation, both spouses are on the same page whereas, with no love, they aren't even in the same library.

Following are some tips that will help you strengthen your relationship:

If your relationship has been over a few rocky patches then it doesn't mean that you are not good enough for your spouse or vice versa. You have probably heard this saying, "Matches are made in heaven." So, one reason you chose your partner could be that you intended it. So, why not think about how your life would have turned out if you didn't have your partner. All those good times where your partner made you laugh, those candlelight dinners, secret birthday surprises, and more... all would be lost.

What would you say to your partner if you knew they were going to be taken away from you in the next moment? A whole picture would flash before your eyes and you will realize that they are the love of your life, have been, and always will be!

Show Your Love

It's easier said than done, right. However, Dr. Orbuch found in her study that men need affirmation. It's hard to fathom that men would want this more than women but the former gender likes to feel special, loved, and cared for. A spontaneous kiss or hug will touch their heart and make them feel warm from the inside.

The psychology behind this is that men neither express nor share their feelings. On the other hand, women do this all the time. They receive positive affirmations from family members and friends every day. This is why a man's thirst for affection is stronger.

Leave the Dishes for a While

Instead of complaining about how it's your turn to do the dishes, why not talk about something upbeat? Your spouse had a hectic day at work. When they come home all tired, you start asking them why they were late, did they have lunch, what happened at the office, etc. Have you ever wondered that instead of asking them anything, how amazing would it be if you offered them a cup of tea with a neck massage?

After that, just leave them be rather than talking about how your day was. This is a huge mood crusher! Our suggestion is to have a happy conversation about anything you have seen them working on for a while. Keep the chat light and breezy and for the love of God, do not talk about finances!

Celebrate All the Good Times

When you were newly married and in your 30s, you used to celebrate every achievement and occasion with your spouse. From when she first said "Yes" to marriage anniversary, birthdays, Valentine's Day, promotion, and more. What about now? Just because you are in your 50s or 70s, it doesn't mean that you aren't allowed to celebrate the good times. Retirement is a huge achievement and it marks the start of a new era so celebrate that.

Your relationship will turn out to be healthier and there will be a few to no resentments. It doesn't matter who starts the tradition, the only thing is that you have to maintain it.

Give Them More Than Your Love

When you reach the Golden Years, your marriage becomes more about trusting than loving each other. There are hundreds of things that keep the motor of your relationship running.

Some of them include understanding, affection, compromise, trust, and acceptance.

- Understand where they are coming from without being judgmental
- Be affectionate with each other, even after a fight
- Compromise when their happiness is bigger than yours. A time will come when they will reciprocate
- Trust that what they are doing is right for you.
- Accept the changes in them and their flaws

Stop Being Clingy

You have been spending time with each other for decades so it's expected to have some sort of dependency on each other. However, when that dependence turns into clinginess, you start to suffocate your spouse. As a result, that crisp freshness you used to have in your relationship starts to dissipate.

People who think that they lose the spark in the later years of marriage are wrong! The more effort you put in, the more your love will build. However, this doesn't mean that you attaché yourself to your spouse's left hip. Here's an example to help you understand this:

A family with a happy kid does not look for validation. Raised by loving parents, he's nurtured in an environment that is warm and open to sharing each other's feelings. This secure attachment allows the kid to cope with any problem and face complex challenges that come his way. Now apply this same situation to a spouse and you will realize that they will feel much more appreciated if you provide them with your love.

Rejection is what makes your spouse seek attachment. While space is important, so is love that helps you bridge the gap between you and your spouse. Feeling secure is important in a relationship because it sets a tone and tells both spouses that they are going strong.

Reasons Why Older Couples Have Healthier Relationships

In movies, you might have often heard the dialogue, "I wanna grow old with you."

Why do people say this? Does this mean that young couples are not happy in their prime years and feel more so when they are older?

Well, in a way... this is true.

A CROP poll that was conducted recently revealed older couples are happier compared to their younger counterparts. 64% of seniors above the age of 55, engaged in a relationship, reported they were content and happy while 56% of the public said the same.

Around 125,000 individuals from different age groups were surveyed and were asked how they felt about the relationship they were currently in and what factors they thought would affect their happiness. People between the ages 65 and 74 said they were happy in their lives alongside their spouse or partner

Seniors listed a number of reasons behind their happiness. As for middle-aged adults, their level of dissatisfaction came from the challenges they faced every day. For example, working full-time jobs, managing a relationship, raising children, etc. On the other hand, seniors have more time to spend on things they love to do. 47% of the public reported that they have to set aside time in order to communicate with their significant other and maintain their relationship.

One of the biggest reasons seniors mentioned that brings them happiness is being empty nesters. Meaning: with no children running around the house or interrupting them, they feel like themselves. This absence of multiple household members allows seniors to pay more attention to their relationships. More importantly, it's the psychological connection that makes the bond more emotionally strong.

For couples to feel truly happy, they need to create a healthy balance between couple time and personal time. A spouse should feel pressured to spend the entire day with their partner and stay focused on them. This is what leads to demands of space, which is not at all productive for the relationship.

Discovering the Lost Spark – Activities for Old Couple to Strengthen Their Bond

Most young couples assume that when they reach the Golden Years, they won't have any trouble in their relationship. That's not true! In fact, older couples face the worst fate and that's having a monotone relationship. All that spark you had when you were married and spent the first few years in absolute bliss… sort of disappears. A routine develops and you seldom stray from this because you think it will cause chaos when in reality, the routine itself is chaotic.

This is why you need a shared hobby that will allow you to bond with your spouse over something that you both love. Who knows, you might end up discovering something new that will change you both. Before we begin, let's have a short Q & A session.

The following questions have been taken from *"The Experimental Generation of Interpersonal Closeness: A Procedure and Some Preliminary Findings."* The experiment has 36 questions, which are to be answered by singles or married couples. According to the results of the study, once all the questions had been answered that were on relationships, death, love, and other topics, several people fell in love and the married ones discovered their lost connection.

1. Given the choice of anyone in the world, whom would you want as a dinner guest?
2. Would you like to be famous? In what way?
3. Before making a phone call, do you ever rehearse what you're going to say? Why?
4. What would constitute a perfect day for you?
5. When did you last sing to yourself? To someone else?

6. If you were able to live to the age of 90 and retain either the mind or body of a 30-year old for the last 60 years of your life, which would you choose?

7. Do you have a secret hunch about how you will die?

8. Name three things you and your partner appear to have in common.

9. For what in your life do you feel most grateful?

10. If you could change anything about the way you were raised, what would it be?

11. Take four minutes and tell your partner your life story in as much detail as possible.

12. If you could wake up tomorrow having gained one quality or ability, what would it be?

13. If a crystal ball could tell you the truth about yourself, your life, the future, or anything else, what would you want to know?

14. Is there something that you've dreamt of doing for a long time? Why haven't you done it?

15. What is the greatest accomplishment of your life?

16. What do you value most in a friendship?

17. What is your most treasured memory?

18. What is your most terrible memory?

19. If you knew that in one year you would die suddenly, would you change anything about the way you are now living? Why?

20. What does friendship mean to you?

21. What roles do love and affection play in your life?

22. Alternate sharing something you consider a positive characteristic of your partner. Share a total of five items.

23. How close and warm is your family? Do you feel your childhood was happier than most other people's?

24. How do you feel about your relationship with your
    mother?
25. Make three true "we" statements each. For instance,
    "we are both in this room feeling..."
26. Complete this sentence "I wish I had someone with
    whom I could share..."
27. If you were going to become a close friend with your
    partner, please share what would be important for him
    or her to know.
28. Tell your partner what you like about them. Be honest
    this time, saying things that you might not say to
    someone you've just met.
29. Share with your partner an embarrassing moment in
    your life.
30. When did you last cry in front of another person? By
    yourself?
31. Tell your partner something that you like about them
    already.
32. What, if anything, is too serious to be joked about?
33. If you were to die this evening with no opportunity to
    communicate with anyone, what would you most regret
    not having told someone? Why haven't you told them
    yet?
34. Your house, containing everything you own, catches
    fire. After saving your loved ones and pets, you have
    time to safely make a final dash to save any one item.
    What would it be? Why?
35. Of all the people in your family, whose death would you
    find most disturbing? Why?
36. Share a personal problem and ask your partner's advice
    on how he or she might handle it. Also, ask your partner

to reflect back to you on how you seem to be feeling about the problem you have chosen.

The goal of this activity is to find out the whimsical things about each other that will make you go, *"Oh, I never thought that you were into…"* There will be a few eye-opening moments that will leave you wondering if you truly know your date, partner, or spouse and that's what this experiment aims to accomplish.

After every question has been answered, you will have a newfound love and respect for your spouse in your eyes and heart that will make you want to spend an eternity with them.

Travel Together

They say that if you truly want to know a person, travel with them. One of the best things about reaching the Golden Years is that you don't have responsibilities. You don't have kids to look after, a job that you need to wake up for early in the morning, commitments that you have made to people, and so on. This means that you can pack your bags any time and go wherever you want to.

Your kids and grandkids probably come to meet you on the weekends so why not dedicate the entire week to an island where you can relax and have poolside drinks? It will just be you and your spouse and no one to interrupt you.

This is why travel is the best bonding activity because it allows you to shed your inhibitions and be your true self.

Have Self-Care Sessions

How does getting a massage with your spouse sound? We can almost hear the blissful sigh that you will be emitting when firm hands will knead your back and melt every bone in your body. If you can't go out then you can make those happy noises at home too… oh Pshhh, you know what we mean.

List down all the comfortable activities you want to try at a spa and then enjoy them with your spouse. Don't forget to take a ton of pictures so that you can go home and remember the recent good times and not just old ones.

Sign Up for a Dancing Class

Why do you think they always show in the movies that a ballroom dance class has old couples? Because it's a sensual activity that brings you closer as a couple. When dancing, you are close to your partner in a romantic manner, which makes love blossom once again between you. It awakens all those dormant feelings that you once had for your partner and simply got lost in time.

The reason why his activity made it onto the list is that it pushes both spouses to maintain a connection. Plus, imagine how amazing you would look at an acquaintance's wedding when you bust out the sweet moves on the dance floor.

Join Other Married Couples

Alright, so what if you are not a fan of taking a walk early in the morning? How about playing Bingo at the community center? Too clichéd. A picnic in the park? A visit to an amusement park and sitting in the teacup ride?

We have given you plenty of options and the point of telling you about them is to enjoy it with your neighbors. You have spent a lot of time by yourself and alone as a couple so why not try different things with a group! If you are an adventurous couple then try parasailing and ziplining at mountain resorts.

Doing something out of the ordinary will strengthen your bond with your spouse and in the process, you will make new friends.

Plan a Game Night

Who said old couples can't enjoy a game night. We aren't going to insult your intelligence by saying Bingo because that's boring. No, we are talking about a gaming adventure, of course not the actual *Game Night* but sort of like the Escape Room.

A friendly game of competition will bring you closer together by keeping you apart. Just don't end up on your spouse's time. Invite your neighbors over and have old-fashioned girls vs. boys night. If it doesn't end well and we do mean this in the best possible way then what's the harm in it. A night of crazy fun, indulging in wine, roaring with laughter with your spouse and friend, and having no worries about tomorrow is what the Golden Years are all about.

Register for a Workshop

Can't find enough time to spend with your spouse? Yes, even in old age this can happen. There are plenty of things that might come in the way such as a personal project you might be working on or a TV series you have been dedicating your spare moments to. Yes, the last one sounds like a sorry excuse but it is what it is.

There's an easy solution to this. Do something that you both like. How about learning a new skill at a workshop? You both can pick your favorite options and enjoy what each other likes. Your willingness to give something your spouse loves a try will not go unnoticed. Keep in mind, when choosing a workshop, go for something that will require two sets of hands rather than one, such as:

- Sculpting
- Sensual baking
- Pottery making
- DIY crafts

Raise a Dog

You are probably wondering what raising a dog has to do with strengthening the bond with your spouse, right. We all know that having a man's best friend by our side makes us a better person. Studies have also reported that people who own dogs have lower stress levels compared to non-dog owners and they are more active.

But, did you know that having a dog makes you more sexually active and attractive? Mind… blown!

According to Astroglide's resident sexologist Dr. Jess O'Reilly, a couple with a dog has increased trust between them. Moreover, they are cooperative, filled with enthusiasm, and have a level of physical intimacy that keeps them bonded. So, go ahead and rush to your nearest dog shelter and adopt a fluff ball now.

Go On a Kayaking Trip

If you love going out on the water then kayaking can be a great way to spend some time with your spouse. The time alone will allow you to talk freely with your spouse. If you have been having fights or bickering a lot then perhaps going on the strip, one where you have coordinated with each other can teach you something new about your spouse.

One thing to notice in these activities is that they are all about bonding. Each one creates room to get to know your spouse differently. Sometimes, watching a movie and cuddling on the couch might be the cure to the rut you are in, and other times, the situation calls for something exciting like changing the scenery and traveling to some exotic place.

What Loves Comes Down to When the Golden Years Begin

What does love mean?

What does life mean?

What does it all mean?

Don't you think if we had the answer to these questions then we might have cracked the code to living a comfortable life happily ever after? If for someone, love is about doing something they are passionate about then it doesn't mean that the same will apply to you.

Love has multiple definitions and the day you discover yours, will be the one when you feel content.

When it comes to marriage, this eternal life question will plague you every now and then. You will try to come up with reasons to make yourself understand but sometimes, things just happen. In the Golden Years, instead of questioning life, you need to seek answers that bring you and your spouse happiness.

That picture-perfect moment of older couples sitting on a park bench, holding hands, talking, and smiling... there's more to it.

Don't you want to enter the late years with your spouse rocking fake teeth and matching canes? Not that things will go down this road… but we are talking about the epic love story of Damon and Elena, the undying devotion Blair had for Chuck, even when he sold her, the belief of Hannah in Dexter, and so on. Why not aspire to be as great as these couples… even though their love was fictional and on screen.

Growing old together is a journey that has many rewards… you just have to reach them. So, instead of giving you more tips on how to bond, let's talk about the lessons of love that will allow you to grow older together and happily.

When You Are Love, Stop Counting the Years… Instead, Make the Years Count

See what we did there? The success of your relationship should NEVER be measured in years. Marriage is not about making your relationship last. It's about enjoying all the moments together and making memories.

Let's count the good days shall we: The moment you first met, your first date, the time when you realized that you love your partner, proposal night, wedding day, birthdays, anniversaries, the day you had your son or daughter, etc. You could create dozens of scrapbooks and still not be finished with the amazing memories that you have created with your spouse.

Couples Who Eat Together, No… Laugh Together, Stay and Grow Old Together

How many times have you heard this saying, "A family that eats together, stays together."

After much thinking, we realized that this does not fall true for older couples. Sure, dinner time brings a family together and allows each member to catch up with what has been happening in their lives but with older couples, this bond is already there.

So, what does it come down to? Laughter!

You will be surprised to know that research has been conducted on this matter and the results are astonishing. According to a study published in the *Journal of Non-Verbal Behavior*, laughter is like a social glue. Shared laughter not only makes people feel good but also allows us to communicate more openly with one another. The study observed the interactions of various people and couples. Those who shared laughter had a similar sense of understanding, which increased the bonding between them and led them to like each other.

The quality of your relationship and its success is measured in happiness. The happier you are, the stronger will be your bond, and the more content you will be in your relationship.

Love Is About Knowing Your Spouse's Imperfections and Accepting Them as Perfect

Even the moon has a little imperfection, yet it is the most beautiful thing in the world. It shines high above and the fact that it's unreachable to us human beings is what makes it more precious. In many folklores, the moon is considered a goddess, her beauty incomparable, who cannot be tamed.

What we are trying to say is that if your spouse has little imperfections then it doesn't mean that you constantly try to change them. Accepting your spouse for who they are is not a compromise. Every person goes through some changes after

marriage. The key to letting those changes affect you and cause
a rift between you and your spouse is to accept them.

This doesn't mean that you go with the flow. A time will come
when they will grow out of their imperfect habits but
remember: they too might not like some of your habits. So, like
we always say — communicate. In the older years, the game
changed a little bit and by now, you have developed the
patience to drown out your spouse's imperfections. If you learn
to do this, there will be nothing left to complain about.

Just... Listen

You fought with your spouse and now you feel like venting out.
So, you call one of your friends and tell them what happened.
They console you, and each one gives you a different piece of
advice. You select the one that feels right to you and then act
accordingly with your spouse. When your spouse reacts
differently, you blame them for the problems and a small fight
over a wet towel turns into this insult match that leads to door
slams.

This is more of a scenario where adult spouses are having it out.
In the case of older couples, things pan out a little differently.
The spouse being blamed will either stand up and leave the
room or call you crazy and then leave the room. In both cases,
lack of communication makes it impossible to solve the matter.

Here's relationship advice 101 — if you have trouble in paradise
then never share your woes with your friends unless they are
there for you only to listen. When you bring friends or family in
the middle of a spat, it becomes difficult to remain unbiased.
Your friends might not fully know the extent of the fight, which
can lead to problems that will be hard to solve later.

Instead of talking with your friends, why not talk with your spouse? If your spouse is a little hot-headed then make them understand that all they have to do is listen. The point of the conversation is not to blame someone but to make the spouse realize that the fight they had could have been easily solved by concluding they both would agree to it.

Getting Old Doesn't Mean You Can't Have a Pillow Fight

We are not telling you to have one of those giggling teen fights but… why not? Has anyone ever told you this: age is just a number? Anytime is a good time to have fun with your spouse, no matter how childish the activity might be. Jump on the bed, eat chips with the crumbs falling everywhere, play a board game, or build a LEGO house. There are uncountable things you can do to bring a smile to each other's faces.

You Don't Always Have to Make a Grand Gesture. Sometimes, a Meaningful Touch Is Enough

A relationship needs nurturing in every way. There was a time when you made grand gestures to impress the love of your life. From proposing to them in a hot air balloon to buying them a diamond bracelet, those were all perfect gestures. However, you don't always have to go big. Yes, they do say, "Go big or go home" but there's something in a meaningful touch that makes your spouse appreciate you more.

Now, what constitutes a meaningful touch?

- Making your spouse coffee because you see them exhausted
- Giving your spouse a massage because they did a late night at the office

- Ordering their favorite food because you saw your spouse looking at a food commercial funny
- Giving your spouse a rose for no reason

Keep in mind that your small gesture should make them feel loved. It's not about the pizzazz but more about how much thought you have put into the idea.

The Recipe for Having a Good Time – Your Spouse, Photo Albums, and a Glass of Wine

Looking at pictures on your mobile phone or laptop is not that intimate. Replace the devices with an actual hardcover album and you have something amazing and memorable. In this day and age, most people go digital and if this is the case with you too then we have the perfect idea: Make a scrapbook.

Ho far back do your memories go? You probably have negatives of the times you were young and met for the first time. So, start with those. For the newer ones, get them printed and then create a timeline. This will be a fun activity that will remind you of all the good times you have had with each other. Perhaps you will remember a funny story that your spouse never knew about, and you both will laugh over it.

Recreate Your Most Cherished Memories

- What are your fondest memories?
- The day you proposed or got proposed?
- The first time your spouse kissed you?
- Your first anniversary?
- That time when you tried skydiving with your partner?
- The first morning after getting married when your spouse brought you breakfast in bed?

How about recreating one of these? Recall the steps you took and make sure that the picture taken at the moment matches the one you took all those years ago. Remember to pick an important thing that made you and your spouse emotional. This will show you how far you have come and what challenges you have faced getting to this point.

Remind Yourself How Boring Your Life Will Be Without Your Spouse

Have you ever wondered how your life would have turned out if you never had met your spouse? If the thought sends you into panic mode then you truly love your spouse. This is not a test but simply a reminder that life, with your spouse, is much more exciting, interesting, and entertaining.

Laughter is the Best Medicine

Every couple reaches the Golden Years after facing plenty of trials and tribulations. A life without painful memories is a life not lived because after pain comes relief and the sense that you accomplished something. With a partner by your side, the journey becomes easy.

How?

Through laughter!

A spouse who can find humor in situations is one you should never let go of. When you reach your senior years, laughing in the face of adversity comes to you naturally. This should be a shining example to young couples that a little humor goes a long way in diffusing any situation.

Start a Tradition

Does your spouse like pancakes in the morning but seldom get to make them?

Do you like to watch the sunrise but always miss it because your spouse has a hectic schedule?

Do you both like watching action movies?

The answer to all these questions is the key to getting closer to each other by starting a tradition. Come up with a routine that you can stick to and then alternate between each other's favorites. Make it "a thing"... sort of a special bonding moment, which defines your relationship.

Family Matters

Just because you are in your Golden Years does mean that you let go of your other relationships. According to a study by Harvard, the secret to living longer is not in genes but joy. The study revealed that embracing community and relationships allows people to live happier and longer.

This is why family is important and you should always make sure that your relationship with your parents, children, and grandkids are intact.

So you see, your relationship is as strong as you make it to be. The more effort you will put in, the happier you will be. Apart from love, happiness, trust, and strong emotions are what strengthen your relationship. Follow these lessons of love and you will see this beautiful change in your relationship that will make your bond unbreakable and eternal.

Conclusion

Love does not have an age limit. It's found and lost in a matter of seconds. You can't just grab the moment by the hands and hold on to it. Sooner or later, love will fade and you will see cracks developing in your relationship.

A healthy and happy marriage is a result of open lines of communication. This is what allows you to reach the Golden Years with a smile on your face. Being in love affects you on a physical and psychological level, this is why they say that *love keeps you young*. A piece of advice that you can give to the younger generation is, "Hang in there. It gets better."

Because it does!

Most people fall in love, form a bond, and get married. This fulfills the "finding a spouse" part of their life. Would you be content with this life flow or would you rather have a bond that is unique and focuses on each other's happiness? As we said earlier, life changes in the most profound way when you get married.

There are uncountable new experiences out there that await you. Relationships differ from couple to couple. While the advice remains the same, the way you choose to act over it is what determines how your relationship will proceed.

As we conclude the love part of this series, here are our parting words:

Tell them how much you miss them... every day, even though they are right by your side

Dare to bare!

No more buts

Act like you just got married

Think about reaching your 70s and having "THE" anniversary

Stop resisting when things take a fun turn

Have your kind of fun by beating the young

Drive them insane… with your love

Let loose your inner child

And lastly, hold on tight because this is it — you loved, you conquered and you are living.